DATE DUE			

Things in My World/
Las cosas de mi mundo

Things at the Park/
Las cosas del parque

Reading consultant/Consultora de lectura:
Susan Nations, M.Ed.,
author, literacy coach,
consultant in literacy development/
autora, tutora de alfabetización,
consultora de desarrollo de la lectura

Please visit our web site at: www.garethstevens.com
For a free color catalog describing Weekly Reader® Early Learning Library's list
of high-quality books, call 1-877-445-5824 (USA) or 1-800-387-3178 (Canada).
Weekly Reader® Early Learning Library's fax: (414) 336-0164.

SP
508
TH1
C-1
9,16

Library of Congress Cataloging-in-Publication Data

Things at the park. Spanish and English.
    Things at the park = Las cosas del parque.
        p. cm. — (Things in my world = Las cosas de mi mundo)
      ISBN-10: 0-8368-7221-5 — ISBN-13: 978-0-8368-7221-7 (lib. bdg.)
      ISBN-10: 0-8368-7228-2 — ISBN-13: 978-0-8368-7228-6 (softcover)
      1. Parks—Juvenile literature. 2. Plants—Juvenile literature. 3. Animals—Juvenile literature.
    I. Weekly Reader Early Learning Library (Firm) II. Title. III. Title: Cosas del parque.
    IV. Series: Things in my world.
    SB481.3.T4518   2006
    508—dc22   2006017285

This edition first published in 2007 by
Weekly Reader® Early Learning Library
A Member of the WRC Media Family of Companies
330 West Olive Street, Suite 100
Milwaukee, WI 53212 USA

Managing editor: Dorothy L. Gibbs
Art direction: Tammy West
Cover design and page layout: Kami Strunsee
Picture research: Diane Laska-Swanke
Photography: Gregg Andersen
Translators: Tatiana Acosta and Guillermo Gutiérrez

Printed in the United States of America

1 2 3 4 5 6 7 8 9 10 09 08 07 06

Note to Educators and Parents

Learning to read is one of the most exciting and challenging things young children do. Among other skills, they are beginning to match the spoken word to print and learn directionality and print conventions. Books that are appropriate for emergent readers will incorporate many of these conventions while also being appealing and entertaining.

The books in the *Things in My World* series are designed to support young readers in the earliest stages of literacy. Children will love looking at the full-color photographs while also being challenged to think about words that name objects and how those words fit into a basic sentence structure. This integration allows young children to maximize their learning as they see how words and ideas are put together.

In addition to serving as wonderful picture books in schools, libraries, and homes, this series is specifically intended to be read within instructional small groups. The small group setting enables the teacher or other adult to provide scaffolding that will boost the reader's efforts. Children and adults alike will find these books supportive, engaging, and fun!

—Susan Nations, M.Ed., author, literacy coach,
and consultant in literacy development

Nota para los maestros y los padres

Aprender a leer es una de las actividades más emocionantes y estimulantes para los niños pequeños. Entre otras destrezas, los niños están comenzando a entender la relación entre el lenguaje oral y el escrito, y a aprender convenciones de la letra impresa como la dirección de lectura. Los libros apropiados para lectores incipientes deben incorporar muchas de estas convenciones, además de resultar atrayentes e interesantes.

Los libros de la colección *Las cosas de mi mundo* están pensados para apoyar a los jóvenes lectores en las primeras etapas de ese aprendizaje. Los niños disfrutarán mirando las fotografías a todo color mientras se les invita a pensar en las palabras que nombran objetos y en cómo esas palabras encajan en la estructura básica de una oración. Esta integración permite a los niños pequeños progresar en el aprendizaje, y los ayuda a entender la relación entre las palabras y las ideas.

Además de servir como maravillosos libros ilustrados en escuelas, bibliotecas y hogares, estos libros han sido especialmente concebidos para ser leídos en pequeños grupos de lectura guiada. El contexto de un grupo reducido permite que el maestro u otro adulto proporcione el andamiaje en el que se basarán los progresos del lector. ¡Estos libros les resultarán útiles, estimulantes y divertidos a niños y a adultos por igual!

— Susan Nations, M.Ed., autora/tutora de alfabetización/
consultora de desarrollo de la lectura

grass

- - -

hierba

I see **grass**.

━ ━ ━ ━ ━

Yo veo la **hierba**.

tree

árbol

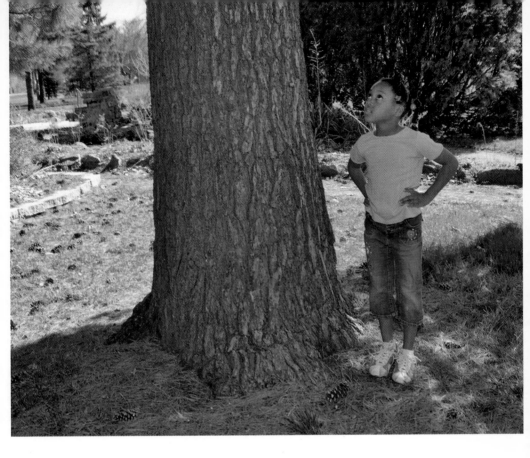

I see a **tree**.

- - - - -

Yo veo un **árbol**.

bird

---

pájaro

I see a **bird**.

▬ ▬ ▬ ▬ ▬

Yo veo un **pájaro**.

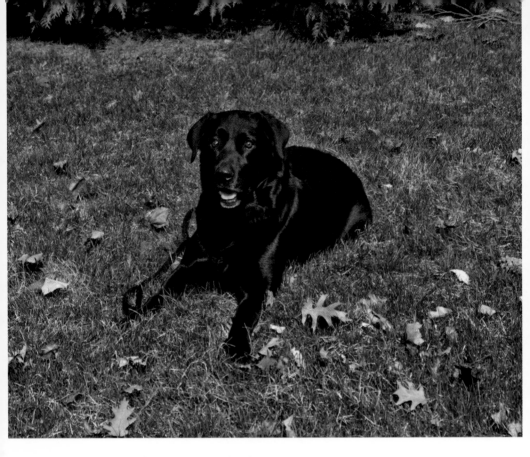

dog

— — —

perro

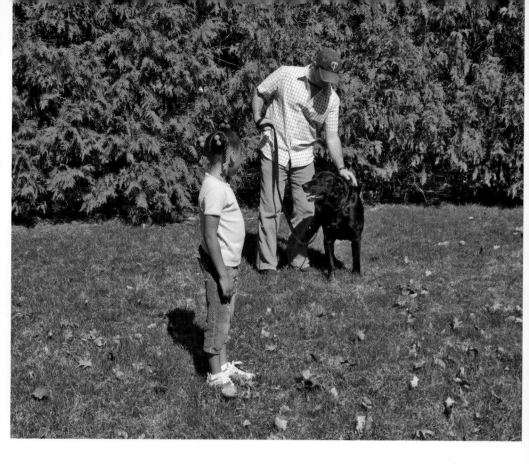

I see a **dog**.

— — — — —

Yo veo un **perro**.

bench

- - - -

banco

I see a **bench**.

Yo veo un **banco**.

slide

- - -

resbaladilla

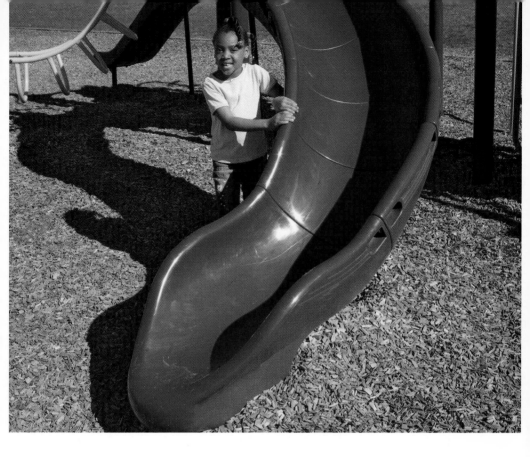

I see a **slide**.

━ ━ ━ ━ ━

Yo veo una **resbaladilla**.

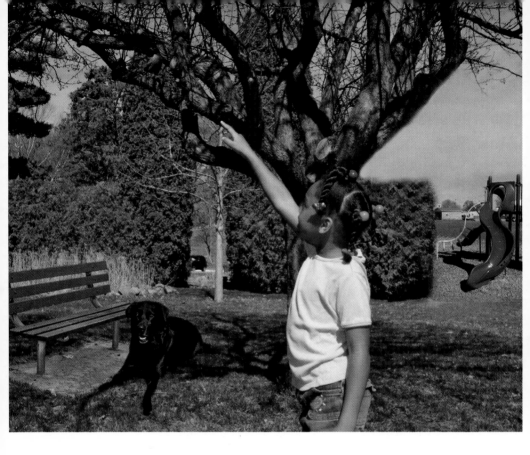

I see many things at the park.

‒ ‒ ‒ ‒ ‒ ‒ ‒ ‒ ‒ ‒ ‒

Yo veo muchas cosas en el parque.